SUCCEED WITH SOCIAL MEDIA

Like a Creative Genius™

A GUIDE FOR ARTISTS, ENTREPRENEURS, INVENTORS, AND KINDRED SPIRITS

BRAINARD CAREY

ALLWORTH PRESS
NEW YORK

Allworth Press books may be purchased in bulk at special discounts for sales promotion, corporate gifts, fund-raising, or educational purposes. Special editions can also be created to specifications. For details, contact the Special Sales Department, Allworth Press, 307 West 36th Street, 11th Floor, New York, NY 10018 or info@skyhorsepublishing.com.

23 22 21 20 19   5 4 3 2 1

Published by Allworth Press, an imprint of Skyhorse Publishing, Inc., 307 West 36th Street, 11th Floor, New York, NY 10018. Allworth Press® is a registered trademark of Skyhorse Publishing, Inc.®, a Delaware corporation.

www.allworth.com

Cover design by Mary Ann Smith

Illustrations by Brainard Carey

Library of Congress Cataloging-in-Publication Data

Names: Carey, Brainard, author.
Title: Succeed with social media like a creative genius: a guide for
   artists, entrepreneurs, inventors, and kindred spirits / Brainard Carey.
Description: New York, NY: Allworth Press, [2019] | Includes index.
Identifiers: LCCN 2019006895 (print) | LCCN 2019009786 (ebook) | ISBN
   9781621537038 (eBook) | ISBN 9781621536987 (pbk.: alk. paper)
Subjects: LCSH: Internet marketing. | Social media.
Classification: LCC HF5415.1265 (ebook) | LCC HF5415.1265 .C3629 2019 (print)
   | DDC 659.14/4—dc23
LC record available at https://lccn.loc.gov/2019006895

Paperback ISBN: 978-1-62153-698-7
eBook ISBN: 978-1-62153-703-8

Printed in the United States of America

This book is dedicated to all my students in Praxis Center for Aesthetics who thrill me daily with their success. Thank you.

♥

CONTENTS

INTRODUCTION

Ah, social media, we hate you! It is an odd relationship we have with so-called "social media." Almost every day we hear of someone saying they are quitting this platform or that one because it is getting in the way of their life. On the one hand, we want our product, our art, perhaps even ourselves, to be known to the world at large, to be "viral" perhaps—and be everywhere at once, resulting in either a wave of profits, or fame, or both.

Industries and individuals everywhere are trying to find the recipe for going viral, or at least getting close to it. It's like the philosopher's stone, the legendary alchemical material that can turn cheap metals like aluminum into gold or silver. It's a bit like a money tree, which is a fantasy of course. Though, with social media, we know a viral hit is real, and it can change a person's life—for real. It is the equivalent of a goose laying a golden egg repeatedly, only you need even less magic—just fingers to type and a phone to make a video, that's all.

In this book I hope to shed light on a real philosopher's stone, the golden goose that we know is possible to use; we just a need a few pointers . . . right? Well, here they are, plain and simple and easy to use, I promise.

There are essentially two methods: 1) free advertising by posting everywhere in the right way with the right content and not paying a dime, or 2) a similar process done with paid ads. Both methods will be discussed and outlined in this book.

If you need more information or support when you're done reading, you can go to likeacreativegenius.com.

We want our product, our art,
perhaps even ourselves, to be known
to the world at large, to be "viral" perhaps—
and be everywhere at once, resulting in
either a wave of profits, or fame, or both.

VIRAL GARBAGE AND YOUR MESSAGE

The love-hate relationship with social media comes from the huge glut of what can be perceived as viral garbage. There are things we want to read and see on social media platforms like Facebook and Twitter and LinkedIn, but there are many things we do not want to see that pollute our stream of information and can alter our mood for the worse. Think of political ads, no matter what party or country they are coming from; they are propaganda designed to sway you with the most vulgar techniques. You have seen inflammatory headlines on which you know you shouldn't click, but you do it anyway because you can't help it. That is called "clickbait," of course, and you and I are the fish that click on it. They have titles like "She's a liar, this video is proof!" or "It's us or him, impeach now!" or even nonpolitical ones, like "Photos that were taken seconds before tragedy struck" or "Ten ways to live a longer life." These are all examples of viral garbage and clickbait, and as abhorrent as this may be, you are competing with them in the vast world of images and text.

We have to begin by thinking about viral garbage, because that trash is the context we are in when we send out our message to the world, be it a product, service, or work of art.

YOUR MESSAGE

The first step in a campaign, about which we will get into detail in every chapter of this book, is to decide on your essential message that will be shared in many different ways.

This may seem obvious, but what most creative people think of as their essential message is in fact often too general and not specific and focused. Here are two examples.

CASE 1: INVENTOR

If you are inventing a new case to cover a mobile phone, it would be easy to think your market is all mobile phone users that have a phone that fits your design. That might be true, but in reality, there are many mobile phone users, and many of them have different tastes. While you think your target market is all phone users, there is only a fraction of those within that market that are your actual buyers. Let's say that you have a cover design that is made out of leather, and users can have it personalized with a monogram if they wish. This type of case can now have a more specific audience—the luxury market for one, because it is more expensive than the average case. Because it can be monogrammed, it is also targeted to a certain class of people, like business executives who might want a monogram. Another unique factor is that the customers who might buy this phone case cannot be vegan, because it is leather. Without going too much further, we already have a focus within a larger market that looks like this: Mobile phone users > Specific model of phone > Luxury market > Business executives > Not vegan. That is now a niche within a niche, one that will be much better in helping you look for customers. So if you are about to launch a Kickstarter project based on that user profile, you now know whom to target in any ads during the campaign, which will save you money and increase sales.

CASE 2: THE ARTIST

If you are an artist trying to sell your art, you might think that the market is very wide—it is anyone that can afford your work and likes it. That is a very broad market indeed, which is not an advantage, because you want to focus on the specific group or groups that will be interested particularly in your art. Let's say your art consists of figurative oil paintings on canvas, and it is often political, satirizing current events. The images tend to be of political figures that are painted to look like crosses between cartoons and animals of various kinds. Sometimes words are added to the paintings. The work tends to satirize conservative causes, like immigration laws and tax benefits for the wealthy. Without going further, let's see what the market is that can be dialed into. It could look like this: Liberal or Democratic voters > Involved in an art organization > Reads the *New York Times* or *Washington Post* > Lives in a major city. Now two of those categories you might think are cutting off too many people (what they read and where they live), but narrowing in those two categories will allow you to spend less money reaching a targeted market that you can then widen in the future.

In short, the best practice is to start with a sharp focus and slowly widen it. I will explain more details of that process throughout the book. Before you move on to the next chapter, please answer the questions on the next page to begin focusing on the demographics of your audience.

CHAPTER 1 TAKEAWAYS

1. What is your product, service, or art?

2. What is your message?

   a. If you are selling a leather case for a phone, it is a luxury message, a lifestyle image that conveys a type of situation and look.

   b. If you are an artist, the message might be your personal story, something specific about the environment, a political issue, or something you are drawn to, like an object or an idea.

3. What is the widest possible audience that would be interested? Think gender, age, and political or organizational affiliations.

4. What does your product, service, or art do for people? (A product usually aids lifestyle; art usually is either decorative or message oriented.)

5. What is the contextual setting for your work? (Products are often used within a specific environment, and art often in the context of a gallery or home.)

**The best practice is to start
with a sharp focus and slowly widen it.**

Chapter 2

LEADERS IN ADVERTISING—GOOGLE, FACEBOOK, AND AMAZON

At the moment, the top ad platforms in the world are Google, Facebook, and Amazon, in that order. The most money is spent on Google, with Facebook coming in second. Amazon comes in a distant third. It is on those top two where you are competing with almost all the viral media on the Internet. Those are also the two places where you can get the most attention and spend money to promote your product or art.

CAMBRIDGE ANALYTICA

In 2018, when Cambridge Analytica was exposed for manipulating Facebook user information for the benefit of advertisers, it provided a case study for advertising and persuading the public to follow a new message. The case was an example of how some of the biggest advertisers (politicians with active campaigns) use social media to send a message and influence behavior. It was also illegal, because they had more information than the average advertiser has access to, but how they spent their money to change the world will prove instructive on how to use these ad giants for yourself.

The firm Cambridge Analytica ran Donald Trump's digital campaign advertising and the campaign for Leave.EU, an organization that was pushing what is now known as Brexit. In hindsight, we know they were fantastically successful campaigns; the United Kingdom did indeed vote to withdraw from the European Union, and Donald Trump became the president of the United States, both seemingly against all odds.

METHODS

After those events, which had real global significance, Cambridge Analytica was no longer allowed to advertise on Facebook, and the company had to dissolve because of legal disputes. But their over-the-top tactics remain a blueprint for anyone who wants real, lasting influence. The methods that can be used for evil can also be used for good. The methodology remains the same for the advertiser—how to reach people and convince them they need to have something they did not know they needed, or how to sway their opinion about an idea or ideology.

The methods used in the political campaigns I mentioned were the ones that many viral video makers use, as do advertisers everywhere—divide and conquer. They generate controversy so that you must take a side: "He's incompetent" or "She's a liar." Then you have two audiences on opposite sides, and you send different messages to each side to persuade them to adopt a point of view about a candidate.

You, however, are making a product or have a service or are an artist, so your message and tactics are a bit different, of course. But if you were a politician, then the Trump presidential campaign would be your model in swaying public opinion through social media!

The next step artists and entrepreneurs have to consider after defining their audience is how to divide that audience up into those who really want what you have versus those who are not interested at all. On Facebook, this process is called "targeting" your audience or "defining" that audience. On Google, it is a similar process. On Amazon, if you are selling products or art, your product will appear near the top of the list when products similar to yours are being searched.

VIDEO CONTENT

In terms of promotion on Facebook and Google, which, unlike Amazon, are arenas where something can go viral, videos have the greatest advantage. By Google, I mean largely YouTube, the video site that is owned and distributed by Google. You have already seen the Gillette ad that went viral (where the company tackles toxic masculinity), or cute animal videos, or the videos of something horrific like a shooting that resulted in death, or videos from self-help gurus that are uplifting. So if you want to make a powerful initial impression, you must think about competing with viral videos by trying to make one of your own. This is a most ambitious yet slippery goal, because there is no recipe for doing so—or is there?

MAKING A VIRAL VIDEO

Some people make viral videos the cheap way—make a compilation of other videos, editing for just the interesting moments, and creating a "best of" video. Or they may do what Gillette did with their ad (which they must have spent a fortune producing): make a video with a message that reflects current social issues and takes a stand—which may alienate many but may also draw in a devoted audience for you and your services or product or art.

A "best of" compilation video might be the closest thing to a guaranteed viral videos. Most are videos that just happen to strike a nerve or make people laugh, and so they are popular. I am talking about them first because you can spend little or no money making these videos, and they will help you to develop your audience and build an online presence. For the rest of this book I will talk about more practical techniques that can get you more visibility online with and without spending money.

As you move through this book, I will discuss various platforms and methods, but here is one basic formula for online recognition and visibility:

1. Make a Facebook Live video → Post it on YouTube → Post to Instagram → Post to Twitter.

2. Promote video as an ad on Facebook.

3. Retarget the people who watched more than 50 percent of the video.

4. Repeat daily or weekly.

In the next chapter, we will discuss how to use this formula in a paid and non-paid version so you can get more branding and visibility for your art, your product, or your service.

CHAPTER 2 TAKEAWAYS

1. List the videos you remember right now without searching for them online.

2. What was your favorite video?

3. Can you think of a way your ideas, art, product, or service can be explained in a video?

4. Have you seen another person similar to yourself making a video that you liked? If so, who made it and what was the video?

5. Can you think of a video you could make that would help your audience understand who you are? If so, what is it?

The next step artists and entrepreneurs
have to consider after defining their audience
is how to divide that audience up into those
who really want what you have versus those
who are not interested at all.

Chapter 3

FACEBOOK LIVE VIDEOS

There are many ways to gain visibility online, but I am focusing on videos right now because it is the dominant form today in which messages are delivered. In later chapters, we will discuss other strategies as well.

Let's begin with the first step in the formula I mentioned:

Make a Facebook Live video → Post it on YouTube → Post to Instagram → Post to Twitter

That is a simple, free, and very effective form of developing an online cross-platform presence. I am sure you are thinking, "But what is a live video and what on earth will I talk about?!"

On Facebook, "live video" is one of the options you can choose when making a post. In the section where you can write a post or post an image, you can also select "live video," and after you choose that, you will have to title your video and, if you like, add a small description to it.

One possible title could be "This is one of my favorite artists: Matisse," and in the description you can say something like, "As an artist myself, I like to share and discuss work that inspires me." A topic like this makes it easy because you are not talking about yourself, and you could do this endlessly.

If you have a product or service, you can discuss the product or talk about other competing products and why some work and others do not, as if you are reviewing products casually. If you have a service like coaching or cutting lawns or cleaning houses, you can give tips on how to do all of those things. I don't mean you should just promote your service; I mean you should make a video about what people can do to cut their lawns better by themselves, or give tips on cleaning, or if you are a coach, give tips on how people can improve their productivity or whatever it is you coach.

Most people don't feel comfortable doing this, so take a deep breath and know you are not alone! Here are ways to enjoy making the video and interact with your audience.

MAKING YOUR FACEBOOK LIVE VIDEO

When you decide to make a video, please understand that you can delete it right away if you really don't like it. You are not stuck with something you truly do not like. The video can be posted on your personal page, but it would be even better if you have a business page attached to your Facebook account and can post it there. There are several advantages to posting it on a business page, which you can easily make no matter what your business or service is, and one of those advantages is that you can promote that video by paying to advertise it.

INTERACTING WITH AN AUDIENCE

I suggest you make a live (not prerecorded) video at least weekly, during the daytime, but don't think too much about what day or time is best. Just make one regularly at whatever time suits you best, on the same day of the week if possible. When making your video, you will begin to draw an audience, and you can see how many people are watching as soon as you begin to record. As you progress through your talk, you can see if people are liking it and that will let you know that your audience is enjoying themselves. While presenting the video, be sure to say that you will answer any questions after it is over. I would suggest keeping the video to about twenty minutes, more or less. Then at the end, you will have the chance to answer questions that will appear in the comments below the video. Now you can speak to your audience directly and answer their questions.

VIDEO PRODUCTION

At first this may sound intimidating if you haven't done this before or are camera shy, but with some practice you'll work out all the kinks. After doing two or three of these, you will see how to interact with comments in real time and will feel more comfortable in front of the camera. The camera, of course, is the one that is built into most laptops, so it will be easy to use. However, there are a few tips to using the computer camera effectively for Facebook Live videos.

1. Keep the camera at eye level. Many amateur videos are made with laptops, and since they are on a desk or table we often see a face looking down into the camera. This has a negative effect on your audience, because it looks like you are literally talking down to them. It also has a very amateur feel to it because we never see videos like that in professional settings—look at how newscasters face the camera, for example. Conversely, if the camera on your computer is too high, it also creates an odd effect of looking up, which is awkward as well. As strange as it may feel, the best practice is to have the camera at eye level and look directly into the camera.

2. Your title and description are important, but don't fret over them too much. Just make the title something clear and descriptive, like "Let's Discuss Matisse." That same title could be adjusted to other artists you talk about. If you cut lawns for a living or are a carpenter, you could say, "Tips for Cutting Your Lawn" or "How to Build a Bird Feeder."

3. The description can be less succinct, but make it brief, such as "A Discussion of Matisse: His Life and Art" or "Five Tips to Improve the Health of Your Lawn" or "Detailed Instructions on Making a Bird Feeder with Three Tools."

Then begin to make your video, and when it is done, you can share it to your other social media sites. The next question—once you get a few of these done and see people reacting and see your audience growing—is whether to keep doing them just like this or start paying for ads to promote them.

I would suggest you keep doing them without spending a dime and see how your reputation grows and what the responses are from your audience. Then you can begin the next steps, if you wish, to begin paying for promotion. In the next chapter we will discuss the rest of this formula for promoting yourself and your art, products, or services by paying for promotion, and also the steps to take for cross-platform attention.

CHAPTER 3 TAKEAWAYS

1. Come up with a subject for your Facebook Live video.

2. Write down a title for the video and a description.

3. Make the video on your business page. (If you don't have a business page, make one.)

4. Be brave and make it at any time of day, any day of the week.

5. After it is done, share the video to your personal Facebook page.

I would suggest you keep sharing content without spending a dime and see how your reputation grows and what the responses are from your audience.

Chapter 4

YOUTUBE

Now that you have made your way through the first part of the social media strategy, which is Make a Facebook Live video → Post it on YouTube → Post to Instagram → Post to Twitter, the next step is to discuss exactly how to post it on YouTube.

It might seem that it is as simple as just downloading the live video from Facebook and uploading it, but there is more involved in this process to be sure the video gets the attention it deserves.

First, you must download that live video from Facebook. At the moment, you can click on the video, and just to the right of the word "Comment" under the right-hand side of the video, you will see three dots •••, and if you click there you will see the option to download that video.

However, Facebook changes how its navigation works regularly, and if you can't find those three little dots, just do a quick search on how to download a Facebook Live video.

Once the video is downloaded, it is time to upload it to YouTube. There are a few things to consider when doing this.

1. Look at the file name, which was probably a meaningless string of numbers and letters when you downloaded it, and change that string of numbers and letters to a few words strung together that have something to do with your video—such as thoughtsonmattise.mp4 or fivetipsforyourlawn.mp4, or whatever your video is about. This helps YouTube searches for that particular topic.

2. Next, you can upload the video to your YouTube channel, a channel that should be dedicated to these types of videos. If you already have a channel with personal videos, then start a new YouTube channel and brand it with your imagery, product, or service by using the visual banners that come with the page.

3. In the description area of the YouTube video, you can really help the visibility of your video by summarizing what you are saying in at least five hundred or more words. This is very important because Google uses these descriptions when people search for something. Search for anything on Google, and you'll notice that each listed result includes a descriptive sentence or two. This text comes straight from the web page, so you need to write something that will make people click on your particular video when you add your description to YouTube. (Tip: If your video is a tutorial, start off with numbered steps so viewers know it will be easy to follow along.)

4. Once your video is uploaded, you can begin to share it on other platforms like Twitter, but there are a few more things to keep in mind about your content on YouTube and why we are doing this.

You might still be wondering why you are posting videos of yourself talking about other artists when you want to share your own art. Or why you are giving tips on cutting lawns, when you just want more work. The answer is about a way of marketing that is often called the 80/20 method. That method dictates that 80 percent of your content should be about things other than what you are selling, and 20 percent should be about what you actually are selling.

So if we take the example of an artist, then you have to share eight videos about other people's art, like paintings by Matisse or a contemporary artist, and then share two videos about your own art. The same goes for services or other products. Share eight videos featuring tips or help for every two videos you share about your own services or products.

VIDEOS ABOUT YOUR WORK: THE 20 PERCENT

The other type of Facebook videos we have not talked about are the ones you produce that are in direct support of your art, your product, or your service.

These are the videos with which you can reach the audience that is now used to getting Facebook Live videos from you and show them what you do.

Starting with an example for an artist, here is the type of live video you could make. I would start with a type of show-and-tell talk. You can explain that you are an artist and that you are in your studio and then show paintings to the viewers by placing them in front of the laptop camera one at a time. Be sure to say after each painting that it is available for sale and to contact you for price inquiries through Messenger. Spend fifteen to twenty minutes on a video like this, and at the end, be sure to say that anyone can message you with any questions.

After making a few videos like this, you might want to make them cleaner and more professional looking so you don't struggle to get the images in the frame, which can feel awkward. One way to do this is to use a software like Open Broadcaster Software (OBS). I am sure that there will be more competitors to this software, but at the moment, it is a free download which allows you to make your Facebook Live videos look more professional. That means you can do things like create a slideshow of images and text to display on the screen. In the video showing off your own art or talking about other people's art, you can use still images that you can size to the screen to show details or zoom out to the full image, and you can also use titles for work or other things you want to highlight using OBS. It is a professional tool that will give your live videos a very impressive feel, and will also communicate your point more clearly.

I would not suggest starting with software like this, but if you are serious about this method of social promotion, then getting that software is the next step to take. It allows you to develop something that can look like a television news broadcast with running text on the bottom of the screen, and many other variations, to make your talk that much more stimulating and effective.

In the case of a service, like a coach or lawn care, the two in ten videos that you make to showcase exactly what you do can also incorporate still images and text. This will make them clear and compelling, as in the example of an artist showing off their work. Not unlike a commercial for a product or service, you can show what you do and let customers know your prices, as well as telling them there is a special discount for those who message you on Facebook and mention the live video.

CHAPTER 4 TAKEAWAYS

1. When your video is finished, download it from Facebook.

2. Change the file name and upload the video to YouTube.

3. Add a summary of five hundred or so words about your video in the description area on YouTube.

4. Post your YouTube video on your personal Facebook page as well as on Twitter.

5. Use the 80/20 method: for every eight informational videos you make, you should only make two that are specifically about your art, product, or service.

Use the 80/20 method: for every eight informational videos you make, you should only make two that are specifically about your art, product, or service.

Chapter 5

RUNNING ADS TO PROMOTE YOUR LIVE VIDEOS

In the past three chapters we have discussed using a specific formula for social media branding, which is: Make a Facebook Live video → Post it on YouTube → Post to Instagram → Post to Twitter. You can do all that for free. If you do it consistently, it will define and promote you and your work. Once this process has started, and you have been doing it for a few months and feel comfortable, you have the option of using advertising to promote the live videos you are making.

FREE PROMOTION

I will explain first how you can promote these videos for free. After you get comfortable with your first live video, you can let people know when the next one is coming up. The easiest way to do this is to make a Facebook Event announcing when you will do your live video. It is easy enough to make an event on Facebook; just look at the top of your personal profile page and to the right of "Friends" and "Photos" you will see a tab for "More"; in that drop-down menu there is a line to start an event. Once you make your event and fill in the details, you can easily share it on your Facebook page and other platforms. You will have a link to the event, which makes it easy to share on Twitter and LinkedIn. Don't hesitate to write a bit about the event and encourage people to come and ask you questions.

ADVERTISING YOUR LIVE FACEBOOK VIDEOS

The other method is to advertise your event on Facebook. As soon as you create your event from your business page, you will see it posted there on the page. Next you can promote your ad by using the button below the post that says "promote" or "boost," and when you click on that button you will have choices for how it is advertised and how much you want to spend.

Advertisers tend to start out very conservatively—for example, spending a total of twenty dollars on the promotion, or ten dollars a day. Depending how far in advance you created the event, you have a few options for your budget. If there are five days until your event starts after you post it, you can either choose a total budget of twenty or thirty dollars or whatever you like, or choose to spend ten dollars a day (which would add up to fifty in total), but either way is fine; just start low and see how it goes.

After setting the budget, you will also have to choose what audience you want the video to go to. Facebook tries to make this an easy process by allowing you to send it to "Friends" or "Friends of Friends" or other groups of people. For your first paid promotion I would suggest you send it to "Friends of Friends" to begin with, or a similar group.

Once you have promoted your Facebook Live upcoming video by advertising it as I just described, you will have some advanced options the next time you do it (assuming more people attend your live Facebook video through the promotion).

What is happening is this: when people attend your live video, you are building an audience, because Facebook remembers who attended (and who actually watched) your live video.

So the next time you promote and advertise your event, you can be sure to advertise to the people who attended previously, but you will also have a series of statistics about who attended. You can see if they were men or women and the percentage of each, as well as their age range and more. Now you can choose to promote to an audience based on some of the statistics you are seeing and also based on their location.

You can advertise your event to people who are only in your local area, or to people who are specifically *not* in your local area. You can advertise to a particular state or country in the world. What you choose depends on what you are talking about in the video. If you are an artist talking about art, and are seeking sales and studio visits, you would want to address people who are geographically local, so that they can visit you. The same would be true if you are offering a service like cutting lawns—you want to work in a specific geographic area, but it might not be your neighborhood; it could be a specific neighborhood near you. If you are a coach and offer a service that can be done by phone, you might want to advertise to your whole state or multiple states and select a gender or age range to define your audience.

Using the idea of paying to drive a new audience to your live event through ads can be a very effective way of reaching an audience and expanding your reach. Since Facebook likes promoting traffic to its own site (as opposed to sending people to an external website) they tend to have lower costs for things like advertising your Facebook Live Event. Whatever you choose to do with paid traffic, take it one step at a time and spend very little to start—like ten or twenty dollars—to test the waters and see what works.

An advanced step is paying for ads is to send special messages with offers of your product only to the people who have watched 50 percent or more of your video, who are considered an engaged audience. Facebook has those statistics, so you can send only those people who watched more than half of the video a special ad that gives them a discount on your services or offers a tour of your studio or an invitation to an exhibition.

CHAPTER 5 TAKEAWAYS

1. Make a Facebook Event on your business page to promote your live video.

2. Share that event on your personal Facebook page as well as Twitter and LinkedIn.

3. When sharing it, comment about it in the post saying why it will be exciting or fun.

4. Try paid advertising for the event by "promoting" it to a small group and spending as little as possible.

5. Use advanced statistics to define and narrow the audience advertised to.

An advanced step is paying for ads is to send special messages with offers of your product only to the people who have watched 50 percent or more of your video, who are considered an engaged audience.

Chapter 6

DESIGNING A SOCIAL MEDIA CAMPAIGN

In the last few chapters I have outlined a specific strategy you can put into practice at no cost or by using paid advertisement. In this chapter and the next one, I will explain another strategy to develop a campaign on which you do not need to spend too much time. In essence, you plan the strategy and the campaign, and then you set it up so it works automatically all week for you.

There are several browser-based solutions to automating campaigns; some of these are Hootsuite, TweetDeck, Buffer, Sprout Social, and Cision. I will give an overview of how to design and implement a social media campaign using these programs.

When you are beginning a campaign, you might think it is measured by how popular your video is or how many likes and comments you are getting. While those are important metrics, they are not nearly important as actually getting a new customer or a strong lead to a new customer—which is an email address in most cases—of someone who is interested.

In our previous discussion on how to develop a basic branding campaign using Facebook Live videos and YouTube, what we didn't discuss was tracking exactly how many clients you get from this process. In other words, how many works of art did you sell and how many new clients for your services did you acquire? The way to begin this process is to define your goals when first designing a social media campaign.

Consider why you are doing this to begin with. Is it to sell more art? If so, which pieces do you want to sell the most, and how many of them? The same goes for any other product or service. How many lawns do you want to cut in a season, and how many new clients are you looking for? In a coaching business, how many clients can you handle, and how many more do you need to meet that goal?

Once that goal is understood, then we can work backward to make your campaign strategy effective. Because likes and shares are not enough to drive your business, you need "conversions," as they are called, otherwise known as sales. Please keep in mind that in most cases, the number of sales you want is not "as many as possible," because you have a finite amount of time, and most businesses can only produce so much, though there are exceptions. For example, an artist can only produce so many works of art in a given year, and only so many lawns can get cut, and only so many clients can be coached in the finite number of hours we all have. Now it is also true that artists can produce limited editions or multiples, and a lawn service can hire more people, and a coach can also hire other coaches and employees to serve more clients—but every business starts with a goal that can be achieved by what some call "the lean model," which means producing a profit without outsourcing and hiring more staff, just you.

So the next step is to define how many customers you can handle right now for the coming year, beginning today. Then ask yourself, how much can you expect each customer to purchase? This is not as easy to determine as it might sound. For example, if you can produce twenty paintings in a year, you may think that is what is available to be sold, but the chances are that some of those paintings will be better than others, meaning some are more popular and more saleable than others, so in fact you might need to produce closer to forty paintings to sell twenty. Be conservative by assuming you need to generate double what you need to sell. The same goes for other products and services. You might think six clients for cutting lawns is good for the season, but some of those clients might stop halfway through. The average coaching client might stay six months, some dropping off in the first month, others staying longer than six months.

Those factors are important in determining your sales goals. At first these are estimates, of course, but they will be refined over the course of working on it all.

The next factor is to determine how many clients you need to make these sales. Again, you must estimate for now. I would initially double the number at least. For example, if you want to sell ten works of art, you need at least twenty people who are seriously interested and discussing the price, and perhaps even more. The same goes for other services and products.

The third important aspect is to research your competition. Who else is selling art, cutting lawns, or coaching clients? Get on their mailing lists. Watch what they do, and see how they run their social media campaigns just by the emails you get from them. That will allow you to analyze what your competition is doing, and also see if they are changing their strategies and in what way.

The final part of developing your strategy is to look over your current profiles and make sure they all reflect what you are trying to achieve. All your profiles should match what your goals are in terms of getting new clients. All your social media profiles should be clear that you are an artist that sells work, or a lawn maintenance company, or a coach of a specific kind, or whatever is that you do or sell.

CHAPTER 6 TAKEAWAYS

1. How many artworks can be sold this year? Or lawns cut, or services rendered, or other product or services you offer?

2. How many clients, approximately, will you need to make those sales?

3. Research your competition. Get on their mailing lists.

4. Analyze your competition and watch for changes in their strategies. Evaluate your previous efforts and determine what works and what doesn't.

5. Update all your profiles on social media so they match your goals.

The final part of developing your strategy is to look over your current profiles and make sure they all reflect what you are trying to achieve.

Chapter 7

AUTOMATING CROSS-PLATFORM CAMPAIGNS

Now that you have a campaign strategy to begin with and know approximately how many clients you need to reach your goals for the year, you can design your strategy around those data. In the previous chapter I laid out the basics of what you need to outline for yourself so you can use software like Hootsuite, TweetDeck, Buffer, Sprout Social, or Cision or the many competitors they have. Some of those are free, like Hootsuite and TweetDeck, and others begin with paid versions, but they are all more or less the same with different bells and whistles. Let's talk about how to use these services to save you time and money.

Essentially, these programs allow you to have a dashboard of all your social media accounts in one place. You can see at a glance what you are posting on each account. For example, if you are about to announce a Facebook Live Event, you can announce that event on every platform you use by scheduling those announcements in advance.

Let's say that your event is happening on Sunday the twentieth of a particular month. You can schedule four announcements leading up to it, and you only have to do it once. You can schedule an announcement of the event on the fifth of the month, then a reminder on the fifteenth of the month, and then a final reminder when you are about to go live five minutes before the event. Those three emails are not only scheduled a month in advance, they are scheduled on all your media platforms, like Twitter, Instagram, LinkedIn, and others.

You will save time and avoid the possibility of missing important posts because you will have all your pages in one place. This system, which all social media managers use, has another advantage, and that is that you can look over all your accounts and see what is working and what is not working. For example, perhaps there were many responses on LinkedIn but not on Twitter, or vice versa. You can also see many more details about who is responding and who is not responding, and more details about those people such as how they saw your post—was it on a mobile phone or computer? And if it was mobile phone, was it an Android or an iPhone? All these data are important because, as we were saying in the last chapter, the goal of all of this social media marketing is very specific—it is to make sales of whatever it is that you are selling. So the more information you have about your customer, the better. Because at one point you will make a sale, or build a relationship with a client, and then you can analyze what happened.

Once you make a sale (or several sales), you can look carefully at how that sale was made and follow its trail through your social media dashboard. As you look at the data you can see patterns. Perhaps you see that people on LinkedIn were the ones that reached out to you through your email, or you might see that when people messaged you on Facebook that you tended to make a sale—and further, that it tended to be people using their phones. Armed with these data you can now adjust your campaign to focus on those areas to be sure that pattern you see is a winning one and is repeated. An adjustment you might make is to focus more on the two platforms that found the best clients for you. If it was through messages that people found you, you can capitalize on this even more so that people are directed to message you.

Remember, you are trying to make sales, so when you see the beginning of a pattern that makes a sale, you need to follow it and do what you can to emphasize that with your social media outreach. This can be done by simply adjusting your posts, changing the wording to appeal to what you know is already working.

PAID TRAFFIC

Just as in our first example of running ads to drive people to your Facebook Live Event, you can also run ads based on the pattern you are seeing through your social media dashboard. So if you are seeing, as in the example above, that certain platforms and certain forms of messaging work best and people with Android phones are responding the most, you can make an ad that will take advantage of this information.

For example, you might run an announcement of a talk you are doing, or you might run an ad that is the recording of the video you made during a Facebook Live Event. Now you can decide what audience to send that ad to. It could be to an audience of a specific age range, which is using an Android phone, and tends to use Messenger to reach you. You can even run your ad within Messenger apps to appeal to those people more quickly.

The amount of data you will get on users is vast, and I have just scratched the surface here in this chapter. You will find out the gender of those who responded, their age range, where they live, what times they are active online, and much, much more. Then you can analyze that based on which people reached out to you and came close to a purchase, and which ones actually made a purchase.

Now you can go back to your dashboard and be even more refined in how you target the best prospects for your campaign. At first it is a matter of trial and error, but soon you will see patterns that you can take advantage of.

The final step is to think about how much each client is worth to you. If it took several ads of a certain kind to have someone reach out and ask the price of your art or your service, then you have a real number to work with. And when you make a sale you have an even better number to work with, because you can eventually see that it costs you, say, twenty-five dollars in ads to get one call or message or a truly interested person, and for every five interested people, you make a sale. That means it costs you $125 to make a sale to a new client. With that information, you can run more ads, knowing you will get a return on your money, so long as the service, product, or art you are selling is worth more than $125.

That is how to use the data you are getting to track when a sale is made, and then repeat the process that made that sale.

CHAPTER 7 TAKEAWAYS

1. Automation is the final step.

2. Use social media dashboard software for scheduling posts.

3. Look at your weekly social media results to see what is working and what is not working, and adjust the next week in favor of the successful content.

4. Track the data (social media posts) and path of your first sale.

5. After the above steps are clear, you can buy ads to automate the path to a sale.

6. Spend no more on the the ad than you make from the resulting sale.

Once you make a sale (or several sales), you can look carefully at how that sale was made and follow its trail through your social media dashboard.

Chapter 8

BUILDING RELATIONSHIPS

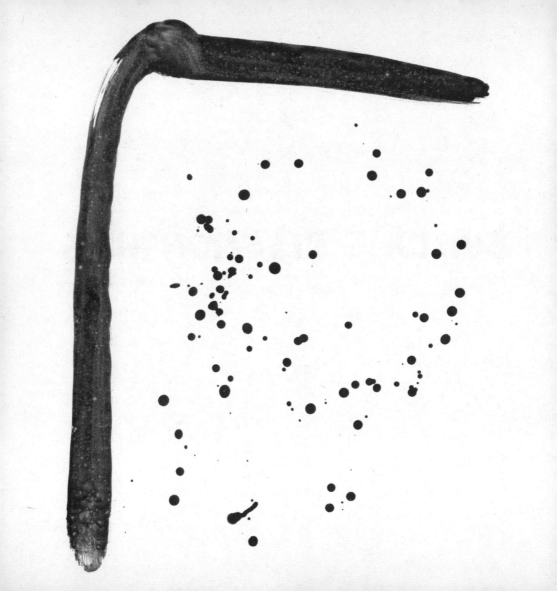

We have discussed Facebook and YouTube quite a bit here, and that is because Facebook has so many users and so much information about those users that it is easy to find your audience, and YouTube is the premier site for videos. But all the other platforms, like LinkedIn, Twitter, and Instagram, are powerful in other ways.

The secret that tends to get ignored is the technique of building personal relationships.

One of the main ways to build relationships on the social media platforms I just mentioned is to comment on posts by other people. You begin by following people who are in your industry. If you are an artist, that means following galleries, museums, and collectors. If you are selling products or services, then follow the people who would be potential clients.

One of the most valuable aspects of social media is building real relationships that are mutually beneficial. The way to create those relationships on LinkedIn, Twitter, or Instagram is to make sincere and thoughtful comments on posts that you see. The way to find interesting posts is to look at your feed of posts by other people whom you are following. If you are following interesting people, this should make for good reading.

Typically posts are scanned and either "liked" or dismissed. The most important part that tends to get ignored is making real comments that the person posting would truly appreciate. This is a tool, a secret, if you will, that tends to get ignored—I have been teaching techniques like this for years, and though I suggest this often, it is rarely used to its full effect.

Imagine you are following a gallery or a museum. When they make posts, you comment on why you like a particular image, and you say something more than "Nice image." You say something thoughtful and even memorable, like "I love this image because it transports me to another world," or "Thank you for posting this; I always felt that this artist was overlooked and deserved more attention." If you are selling products or services, you can comment in similar ways on accounts of people you want to work with.

Everyone reads comments that appear on their posts, and when they get a compliment, the first thing they do is click on the link of the profile of the person who made the compliment, because they want to know who this person is. Boom, you are on their radar, just like that.

I am not sure why this advice usually goes unheeded. Perhaps because it takes time, and it must be real and sincere. In all the chapters before this one, I have explained ways in which you can create a campaign to reach your ideal customer, and even automate part of that, but that whole process is different from building relationships one person at a time. Both are valuable, yet I find most people are interested in the large-scale campaign and not in the one-on-one interaction. I am not sure why this is, but I strongly urge you to use this one-on-one method in equal measure, because one relationship can get you very far.

ONE-ON-ONE RELATIONSHIPS

Besides commenting on posts in your newsfeed on Twitter, LinkedIn, and Instagram, you can also direct message people in many cases and build a personal relationship from there. There is a platform I use called Alignable, which is another social media service that allows businesses to connect with one another and make referrals. I suggest you look at it and consider joining, but I mention it mainly because they have an interesting reply system. When someone wants to connect to you, and become a "friend," there are a few replies that you can just click a button to send, and one of those is "Let's meet for coffee." That struck me, because it is what I am talking about here when I suggest pursuing real relationships. I am not the first person to realize the importance of building real relationships through social media, and this platform in particular encourages us to reach out and meet people somewhere for coffee. Again, this may be the one piece of advice from this book that you will not pursue, but it is the most important of all.

If you are an artist, you want real relationships with collectors who come to your studio and talk to you. If you are cutting lawns, you want your customers to trust you and feel comfortable working with you. And if you are selling a service like coaching, you want to have the trust of the client you are working with. All of that can be started through the social media tactics that I mention in the first six chapters of this book, but it must end with a real relationship, which is what I am discussing in this chapter.

Meeting for coffee is a great way to start a relationship that may or may not be mutually beneficial. Relationships are chemistry; sometimes they work and sometimes they don't, but you will never know unless you are face-to-face with someone. You don't need to have an agenda when you are meeting someone; you can just ask for a meeting to discuss your mutual business, and most people will willing to meet. After all don't we all want some new friends that might make our day and our business a little brighter?

It's interesting how a meeting can go. Once I noticed someone liked a tweet of mine on Twitter and said, "Wow, that's cool!" about some art I posted. The first thing I did, and the first thing most people do when they get a compliment, as I said previously, was to click on the profile of the person who complimented me. That is why compliments work so well—we all want to know who this person is who just gave us a compliment. In the case I am mentioning, I clicked on that person's profile and saw that he was a creative director at the design firm Saatchi & Saatchi. I was impressed and direct messaged him and asked him if he wanted to have a coffee.

I had no idea what would happen in the meeting. I asked him about what he was doing, and we chatted for a while. Often, the person you are meeting would like the meeting to be beneficial to both of you. It's human nature that we want to help each other, and we don't want to waste our time. I'm not saying every meeting will be a win, but the odds are tilted in your favor. At the meeting with the creative director, he said toward the end, "I have an idea—I will have my team design all your materials, website, cards, everything, all pro bono." He offered to do all the design work for anything I wanted for free! For the creative director, it was a side project that his team could have fun with and possibly snag a design award. That was a win, and I have kept in touch with him ever since. The same can happen to you and your business in many other forms if you use social media as a means to find interesting people to join you for coffee.

CHAPTER 8 TAKEAWAYS

1. Follow people and organizations that you want to work with on Twitter, LinkedIn, Instagram, and Facebook.

2. Make thoughtful comments on their posts—not just likes and two-word comments.

3. Reach out to people and make comments through direct message.

4. Suggest a meeting over coffee to discuss your businesses.

5. Have that coffee meeting with no agenda, just to learn about the other person.

Meeting for coffee is a great way to start a relationship that may or may not be mutually beneficial. Relationships are chemistry; sometimes they work and sometimes they don't, but you will never know unless you are face-to-face with someone.

Chapter 9

WRITING CONTENT FOR GENERATING NEW CUSTOMERS

As you can see, there are several approaches to social media management and ways of branding yourself online to get your message and product in front of the right eyes. As much as this all can seem like digital wizardry—following all the metrics of how your campaign is running to determine whom you are reaching and the cost of securing one customer—that is exactly what all the online businesses that stay in business are doing. They are looking over the numbers of who showed interest and how much it took to get one sale, and then they try to reproduce that pattern. We have gone over a few ways to create that pattern so you can do it for yourself, but there are always more ways to reach customers. I will explain one more that is very popular.

WRITING ARTICLES

There is a method of bringing people into your pattern of acquiring a customer, a method that is slightly different from the rest but one you have probably seen. It is a post on social media platforms that looks like a link to an article. I am sure you have clicked on many articles, when you have seen a headline or the first sentence, on Twitter, Facebook, or LinkedIn. When you click on that link you are of course taken directly to the article, which you begin to read. Often it has a few pictures in it. This is very effective because the article is real content that you want to read, and it will hopefully open your eyes or your mind to something that sparks your interest.

The way to use this behavior of reading articles on the Internet is to write an article yourself and put it on a page on your website, or make a landing page, which is a webpage that stands on its own. Put a heading at the top that could identify your business, but keep it low-key so that it actually looks like an article that takes itself seriously and is not just about your business.

For example, if you are an artist, the heading could be something about art that isn't you or your brand, like Collecting Art Digest, or Collectors Quarterly. Then you can write an article about best practices for collecting art. I would write at least five hundred to eight hundred words and make it a useful piece about how to collect art and what to look for when deciding on the right art to collect. If you are unsure what to write, you can search other articles on the same topic for inspiration. Then at the bottom of your article, have a call to action such as, "Would you like to know more about collecting art? Then sign up here" and include a sign-up form.

This kind of content is easy to share and does not look like you are selling something, and is an easy way to establish your expertise and collect emails from the right kind of client, which you can then follow up on. This same method could be used for any industry, of course—writing articles that share good information, and at the end an offer to send them more information if they sign up to your mailing list.

This type of outreach is very successful as a paid and non-paid ad. Because we all want new information that is genuinely useful, rather than just an ad that leads to an offer, this is a method that allows the reader to begin to trust you, which is the heart of any new relationship.

CHAPTER 9 TAKEAWAYS

1. Write an article on an aspect of your industry.

2. Use a header on the top of the article that reads like a news journal of your industry.

3. At the end of the article, allow the reader an opportunity to sign up to your mailing list.

4. Email the reader regularly about your business and tell them when you are having live Facebook talks or similar events.

5. Share this without spending money, and if it gets comments and likes, run it as an ad on the social media of your choice.

AFTERWORD: WHY FRIENDS MATTER

The importance of face-to-face meetings cannot be emphasized enough here. You can use any of the techniques in this book or use different new techniques, or make up your own, but in all industries from artists to coaches to inventors, one-on-one relationships are the most important factor in building a network of support, and that begins with a face-to-face meeting with people you don't know. The way you meet these people is to follow them on the social media of your choice, comment on their posts if they are saying something interesting, and then ask them for coffee near where they live. Some will say yes, and some will say no, of course.

But don't we all want more friends as well as customers for our business? Social media is a way to meet people with the least possible effort. No need for cold calls or awkward meet-up groups; now we have the ability to explore the ideas of potential friends first and reach out by commenting when we are comfortable. What could be easier? What could be a safer way to meet someone? This is the new way we make friends and develop relationships with potential customers.

I wish you great success in the realm of social media, which means I wish you an abundance of real friends, a real community of support, as well as customers and clients with whom you will have sincere and mutually beneficial relationships.

If you want to hear more from me, I can be found on social media, and you can also hear more from me by going to my website and signing up for my latest news at likeacreativegenius.com.

I wish you well!

For more support, watch the videos on
likeacreativegenius.com.

SUGGESTED READING

If this book got you excited,
there are lots more to read
to get more angles on the
process of selling online. Here
are some that I recommend.

The Art of Social Media—Guy Kawasaki and Peg Fitzpatrick

Crushing It! How Great Entrepreneurs Build Their Business and Influence—and How You Can, Too—Gary Vaynerchuk

Fund Your Dreams Like a Creative Genius™—Brainard Carey

Growth Hacker Marketing—Ryan Holiday

Influencer—Brittany Hennessy

LinkedIn Unlocked—Melonie Dodaro

One Million Followers—Brendan Kane

Permission Marketing: Turning Strangers into Friends and Friends into Customers—Seth Godin

Sell Online Like a Creative Genius™—Brainard Carey

This Is Marketing—Seth Godin

To Sell Is Human—Daniel H. Pink

Trust Me, I'm Lying—Ryan Holiday

YouTube Secrets—Sean Cannell and Benji Travis

The Zen of Social Media Marketing—Shama Hyder

INDEX

Books from Allworth Press

The Art World Demystified
by Brainard Carey (6 × 9, 308 pages, paperback, $19.99)

Brand Thinking and Other Noble Pursuits
by Debbie Millman with foreword by Rob Walker (6 × 9, 336 pages, paperback, $19.95)

Branding for Bloggers
by Zach Heller with the New York Institute of Career Development (5½ × 8¼, 112 pages, paperback, $16.95)

Feng Shui and Money (Second Edition)
by Eric Shaffert (6 × 9, 256 pages, paperback, $19.99)

From Idea to Exit (Revised Edition)
by Jeffrey Weber (6 × 9, 272 pages, paperback, $19.95)

Fund Your Dreams Like a Creative Genius™
by Brainard Carey (6⅛ × 6⅛, 160 pages, paperback, $12.99)

Making It in the Art World
by Brainard Carey (6 × 9, 256 pages, paperback, $19.95)

Millennial Rules
by T. Scott Gross (6 × 9, 176 pages, paperback, $16.95)

The Money Mentor
by Tad Crawford (6 × 9, 272 pages, paperback, $24.95)

The Online Writer's Companion
by P. J. Aitken (6 × 9, 344 pages, paperback, $19.99)

The Profitable Artist (Second Edition)
by The New York Foundation for the Arts (6 × 9, 288 pages, paperback, $24.99)

The Secret Life of Money
by Tad Crawford (5½ × 8½, 304 pages, paperback, $19.95)

Sell Online Like a Creative Genius™
by Brainard Carey (6⅛× 6⅛, 160 pages, paperback, $12.99)

Starting Your Career as a Professional Blogger
by Jacqueline Bodnar (6 × 9, 192 pages, paperback, $19.95)

Website Branding for Small Businesses
by Nathalie Nahai (6 × 9, 288 pages, paperback, $19.95)

To see our complete catalog or to order online, please visit www.allworth.com.